Birth

of the

Chosen One

Listen to the Christmas Story Again for the First Time!

Retold by
Terry M. Wildman

Great Thunder Publishing

Birth of the Chosen One
Retold by Terry M. Wildman
© 2013 Terry M. Wildman

Great Thunder Publishing, Maricopa, Arizona

ISBN 978-0-9847706-2-5

Image editing and front and back cover design, Mark Sequeira, MJA Studios

The text of this book is adapted from the First Nations Version Project by Terry M. Wildman. This version may differ slightly from other editions of the First Nations Version.

Author's Introduction

This is the story of the birth of Jesus retold from the Sacred Book called the Holy Bible.

I present this story in the tradition of the oral storytellers from our many Native American cultures. This telling is not intended to be culturally or tribally specific but to relate in a general way to Native Americans and other First Nations people.

The names used in this story reflect the meanings of the names in the original languages of the Bible.

The text for this story is taken from *First Nations Version Project* by this author. You can read about this project in the back of this book or visit www.firstnationsversion.com.

This retelling is personal, as it reflects my own experiences and perspectives. To present the scriptures as a living and moving narrative I sometimes added reasonably implied statements. For this I used my imagination and took a few liberties as I tried to picture what might have been the response of the participants. These portions are *italicized;* they are not meant to add or take away from the meaning of the Sacred Scriptures.

This story is for children of all ages—enjoy!

Terry M. Wildman, Ojibwe and Yaqui Heritage
Gitchi Animiki Meno Mashkiki Manidoo
Voice of the Great Thunder with a Good Medicine Spirit

First Words

Long ago, in many ways and at many times, the Great Spirit spoke to our ancestors through holy men and prophets.

But now, in these last days, when everything is to come full circle, he has spoken to all people through his son, the one he has chosen to give all things to. It is through his son that the One Above Us All made the world that is, the world that was and the one that is coming.

He is the light that shines from the Great Spirit's face and represents him in every way.

It is his powerful Word that holds the stars above, the earth below and all things seen and unseen in their place.

Ancient Prophecies

Listen to the words of holy men of old as they spoke of a time when the Maker of Life would send his Chosen One to restore all things.

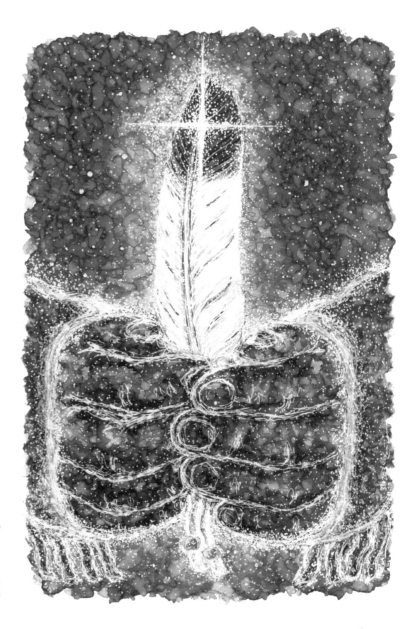

"A small one has been born for us, a son has been gifted to us. The guidance of all people will come to be on his shoulders. He will be called Wisest of Elders, Great and Powerful Spirit, Grandfather from the Place Beyond Time, Grand Chief of Peace. His guidance of peace and harmony will reach farther than the eye can see and will last longer than the end of all days."

"The One Above Us All will give us a sign. A young virgin will be with child and give birth to a son. His name will be known as Creator is With Us."

"Bethlehem, O House of Bread, also called Fruitful Place. Even though you are small among the clans of the Promised Land, from you the Great Spirit will send one who will be Chieftain of the tribes of Wrestles With Creator. One who comes from long ago, from the ancient days."

This is the story of the birth of the Chosen One, retold from the Sacred Book, the greatest story of all!

It began over two thousand years ago in the land of the tribes of Wrestles With Creator.

At the Right Time

For many generations powerful nations had ruled the land surrounding the tribes of Wrestles With Creator. The most recent were the People of Iron, called Romans. This government took control of the tribes and dominated them for nearly two generations.

They forced their treaties on the tribes, but allowed some freedoms. They could practice their own spiritual ways, build gathering houses, and maintain a Sacred Lodge to perform their ceremonies and make their prayers.

This government also allowed them to have their own tribal chiefs. But over many years some of these chiefs became corrupt and were controlled more by the ways of the People of Iron than their ancient Sacred Ways.

The people were oppressed and feared this powerful government with its many soldiers and weapons of war. They kept praying and hoping that the Great Spirit would fulfill the age old prophecies and send the Chosen One, a great warrior chief, who would set them free.

This was the way of things, in those days, for all the tribes of Wrestles With Creator.

CREATOR REMEMBERS
HIS PROMISE

It was in the time of the bad hearted Chief Looks Brave, who ruled the Promised Land, that Creator chose to send a powerful spirit messenger to Jerusalem, the sacred village of peace, to a holy man whose name was Creator Will Remember.

He and his wife, Creator is My Promise, were both descended from the tribe of priests. They had deep respect for the Great Spirit. With good and pure hearts they walked a straight path, staying true to the tribal ways and traditions given them by the Great Spirit. They lived in the hill country, in the Promised Land of the tribes of Wrestles With Creator.

But Creator is My Promise was barren, unable to have children, and they both were growing old in years.

Creator Will Remember belonged to a priestly clan that shared the responsibility of performing prayers and ceremonies in the Great Spirit's Sacred Lodge that was in Jerusalem.

He was chosen, in the traditional way, to be the one to enter the lodge and perform the sweet smelling smoke ceremony for the evening prayer. A large number of people gathered outside to pray while he went inside to perform the ceremony.

As the smoke went up with his prayers, suddenly a messenger from the Great Spirit appeared to him, standing to the right of the altar of incense.

Creator Will Remember was troubled when he saw the spirit messenger. He trembled with fear *that covered him like a blanket.*

"Don't be afraid!" the messenger said to him.

"Your prayers have been heard. The Maker of Life will give you and your wife a son. You will give him the name Creator Shows Goodwill. He will bring great joy to you, and many people will be glad that he has been born."

The aroma of the sweet smelling smoke filled the Sacred Lodge as the messenger continued.

"He will be great and honorable in Creator's sight. He will not taste strong drink or wine. Even in his mother's womb he will drink deeply of the Holy Spirit. He will help many of the children of the tribes of Wrestles With Creator find the good road and return to the Great Spirit's ways."

Creator Will Remember stood silently. His whole being continued to tremble as the messenger finished.

"He will prepare the way for the Chosen One, walking in the same spiritual powers of the holy man and prophet of old, whose name is Great Spirit is Creator.

"He will turn the hearts of many fathers toward their children, and many rebellious children will again honor the wisdom of their elders; so that people will be ready to participate in Creator's plan."

When the messenger finished speaking, his words echoed through the Lodge. Still trembling Creator Will Remember finally found his voice.

Then he questioned the messenger, "We are too old to have children, how can I believe your words?"

The spirit messenger replied, "My name is Creator's Mighty One, his chief messenger, I stand close to the Great Spirit! I was sent to speak these blessing words to you, and they will come to pass, but because you did not believe my words, you will not be able to speak until they are fulfilled."

The people who were praying outside began to wonder why it was taking so long for Creator Will Remember to come out of the Lodge. When he finally came out, unable to speak and not saying a word, but making signs with his hands, they understood that he had seen a vision.

When the traditional ceremonies were finished he returned to his home in the hill country. Soon afterward Creator Is My Promise was with child. She stayed at home and for five moons did not show herself to anyone.

She said in her heart, "The Giver of Breath has poured out his blessing ways on me! He has taken away my shame. Now I will have respect in the eyes of my people."

BITTER TEARS

When six moons had passed the Great Spirit sent the same spirit messenger, Creator's Mighty One, to another small out of the way village in the hill country called Nazareth.

There he appeared to a young virgin woman named Bitter Tears, who was promised in marriage to a man named He Gives Sons, a descendant of the great chief Much Loved One.

Creator's Mighty One said to her, "Greetings, highly favored one! You are close to the Great Spirit and greatly honored among women."

Bitter Tears was deeply troubled by this greeting and wondered what the spirit messenger would say.

"Don't be afraid," he said, "for you have found good will in the eyes of the Great Mystery. You will be with child and give birth to a son; you will call him Creator Sets Free."

It seemed like time stood still, and all creation paused to listen, as the messenger continued to speak.

"He shall be a greatly honored one, the son of the One Above Us All. He will be Grand Chief like his ancestor Much Loved One and will sit in his place of honor. He will always be chief over the tribes of Wrestles With Creator. His chiefly guidance will never end."

Bitter Tears' voice trembled with emotion, and her eyes grew wide as she looked into the face of the spirit messenger.

She asked, "How will this be, since I have never been with a man?"

Creator's Mighty One replied, "The Holy Spirit will spread his wings over you, and his great power from above will overshadow you. This Holy Child born to you will be the son of the One Above Us All."

To encourage her he said, "Your cousin Creator is My Promise, who was called barren one, is six moons with child. There is nothing too hard for the Great Spirit!"

She looked into the face of the messenger, with a small tear in her eye and bravely declared.

"I am Creator's servant. Let it be for me just as you have said." Then Creator's chief spirit messenger left her.

Cousins

Bitter Tears quickly put together a traveling bundle and went to visit her cousin in a nearby village. When she entered the home of her relatives she greeted her cousin, Creator is My Promise. When she heard Bitter Tears' greeting she felt her child jump inside her. She was filled with the Holy Spirit, and with a loud cry she lifted her voice and spoke these blessing words to Bitter Tears.

"The Most Holy One has honored you more than any other woman! The child you carry inside you will bring blessing ways to all people. Why is Creator being so kind to me, sending the mother of the Great Chief to visit my home?

"As soon as I heard your greeting my baby jumped for joy inside me! You have been chosen by the Maker of Life for a great honor, because you believed his words to you."

Bitter Tears was full of gladness and her words flowed out like a song.

"From deep in my heart I dance with joy to honor the Great Spirit. Even though I am small and weak he noticed me, now I will be looked up to by all. The Mighty One has lifted me up! His name is sacred, he is the Great and Holy One."

Her face seemed to shine as she continued.

"He shows kindness and mercy to both children and elders who respect him. His strong arm has brought low the ones who think they are better than others. He counts coup with arrogant warrior chiefs but puts a headdress of honor on those of a humble heart."

She smiled, looked up to the sky, and shouted for joy!

"He prepares a great feast for those who are hungry, but sends the fat ones home with empty bellies. He remembers the promise he made to the tribes of Wrestles With Creator and has shown kindness to the children of Father of Many Nations."

When she finished speaking they both laughed with joy. With hearts full of gladness they told each other their stories.

For three moons Bitter Tears stayed in the home of her cousin and then returned to her own village.

A Promise Fulfilled

When her time came Creator is My Promise gave birth to a son. When her relatives and close friends heard the good news, that the Great Spirit had been so kind to her, they were glad and rejoiced!

Then, eight days later at his naming ceremony, all the relatives wanted to name him after his father.

"No," she said to everyone's surprise, "his name will be Creator Shows Goodwill!" But they said to her, "No one in your family has that name." They made signs with their hands to Creator Will Remember to see what he wanted to name him. He asked for a writing tablet and to their surprise wrote, "His name is Creator Shows Goodwill." Suddenly he could speak again and began to thank the Great Spirit out loud.

Then, with a glad heart, he spoke these words that the Holy Spirit was giving to him to say.

"All blessing ways to the Great Spirit of the tribes of Wrestles With Creator! For he has come to rescue his people from a great captivity. In the land of our ancestor, Much Loved One, he has lifted up his coup stick to show his great power to help us."

He lifted trembling hands to the sky and cried out.

"He has remembered his ancient promises, made to our ancestors since the beginning of time, and the peace treaty he made with Father of Many Nations.

"He has come to set us free so we can walk in his good and sacred ways without having to fear our enemies who surround us."

Then he turned to his newborn son and with warm words spoke these blessing words to him.

"And you, my son, will be a holy man from the One Above Us All. You will make a clear path for the coming of the Grand Chief, to show his people that he will help us by cleansing us from our bad hearts and wrongdoings."

"Because Creator is kind and gentle, he will come to us as the sunrise from above, to shine on the ones who sit in darkness and in the land of death's shadow, to guide our feet on the good road of peace."

All the people who heard about this were filled with wonder. Throughout the hills and valleys of the Promised Land they began to speak about what they had seen and heard. All who listened began to say to themselves, "This child must have been born for some great thing."

For it was clear that the Great Spirit's hand was upon him in a powerful and good way. Creator Shows Goodwill grew strong in body and spirit and stayed in the desert, waiting until the time was right to show himself to the tribes of Wrestles With Creator.

DREAM GUIDANCE

Bitter Tears had returned home to be with her family and to He Gives Sons, the man she was promised to in marriage. Before they came together he discovered that she was with child. Because he was a man of honor and did not want to disgrace her, he thought about secretly releasing her from the marriage promise.

As he wondered about these things, a messenger from the Great Spirit appeared to him in a dream, and said, "He Gives Sons, son of Much Loved One, do not be afraid to take Bitter Tears to be your wife, because the father of the child is the Holy Spirit."

The dream ended with these words from the spirit messenger.

"She will give birth to a son, you will name him Creator Sets Free, because he will set his people free from their bad hearts and wrongdoings."

This fulfilled the words spoken long ago by the prophet, "A young virgin will be with child and will give birth to a son, they will call his name Creator is With Us."

When He Gives Sons awoke, he followed the guidance given him in the dream and took Bitter Tears to be his wife. But he did not have relations with her until after the child was born.

Humble Birth

When the time drew close for Bitter Tears to have her child the government of the People of Iron ordered that a census should be taken. All the people were required to travel to their ancestral homeland to register.

He Gives Sons and Bitter Tears set out on a long journey to Bethlehem the village of their ancestor Much Loved One, the great chief.

The journey took several long days and cold nights as they traveled over high hills and through the dry desert. When they arrived tired and weary, they entered the crowded village.

The time for Bitter Tears to have her child was upon her! But no place could be found in the lodging house, so He Gives Sons found a stable where it was warm and dry. There she gave birth to her son. They wrapped him in a warm soft blanket and *laid him on a baby board.* Then they placed him on a bed of straw in a feeding trough.

That night, in the fields nearby, sheepherders were keeping watch over their sheep. Suddenly a great light from above was shining all around them. A spirit messenger from Creator appeared to them. They shook with fear and trembled as the messenger said to them, "Don't be afraid, I bring you good news that will be for all nations. Today in the village of Much Loved One a great chief has been born, he is the Chosen One!"

The messenger continued, "This is how you will know him, you will find the child wrapped in a blanket and lying in a feeding trough."

Suddenly a great number of spirit warriors appeared giving thanks to Creator saying, "All honor to the One Above Us All and on the earth let there be peace to all who stay under the shadow of his wings."

When the spirit warriors returned to the world above the sheepherders said to each other, "Let us go and see this great thing the Creator has told to us." So they hurried to the village of Chief Much Loved One and found the child just as they were told, lying in a feeding trough!

They left with glad hearts and began to tell everyone what they had seen. All who heard their story were amazed.

The sheepherders returned to their fields, giving thanks to the Great Spirit for the wonders they had seen and heard.

Bitter Tears kept all these things hidden in the medicine pouch of her heart and wondered what all this would mean.

Keeping

The Traditions

After eight days, at his traditional naming ceremony, they gave him the name, Creator Sets Free. The name given by the spirit messenger before the child was born.

Then, about one moon later, the time came for them to present their child to the Great Spirit. This was their purification ceremony, an ancient tradition from the great law giver Drawn From the Water, who said, "Every male child who is first to open the womb will be holy in the Great Spirit's sight. Bring two turtledoves or two young pigeons to be burned with fire as a sweet smelling smoke offering."

They journeyed to Jerusalem to the Great Spirit's Sacred Lodge for this ceremony.

When they arrived they were welcomed by Creator Hears, a holy man who did what was right in the Great Spirit's sight and waited patiently for him to fulfill his promises to the tribes of Wrestles With Creator. The Holy Spirit rested on him and told him that he would not die until he saw Creator's Chosen One with his own eyes.

As Creator Hears followed the guidance of the Spirit he arrived at the Sacred Lodge just in time to see He Gives Sons and Bitter Tears bringing their child for the purification ceremony. Creator Hears took the child into his arms and spoke blessing words over him.

"O Great Father, I now see with my own eyes the one you have prepared for all Nations. The one who will set us free from our bad hearts and wrongdoings. He will make a clear path for all people to see and bring honor to the tribes of Wrestles With Creator. Now, just as you have said, I can cross over in peace."

The child's father and mother were amazed at what was being said. So Creator Hears spoke blessing words over them also.

He then turned to Bitter Tears and spoke softly in her ear.

"This child has been chosen for the fall and rising of many in the tribes of Wrestles With Creator. He will be a sign that will be spoken against, so the hidden thoughts of many hearts will be seen."

His voice softened as she looked sadly into his eyes.

He said to her, "Even your own heart will be pierced through like a sharp arrow."

As they pondered his words a holy woman named Shows Good Will, a tribal elder of many years, welcomed them. She stayed at Creator's Sacred Lodge night and day with fasting and many prayers.

When she saw the child she gave thanks to the Great Spirit and began to tell about the child, to all who were waiting for Creator to fulfill his promises to Jerusalem, the sacred village of peace.

WISDOMKEEPERS

After the Chosen One's birth in Bethlehem, Wisdomkeepers traveling on a long journey from the East, came to Jerusalem.

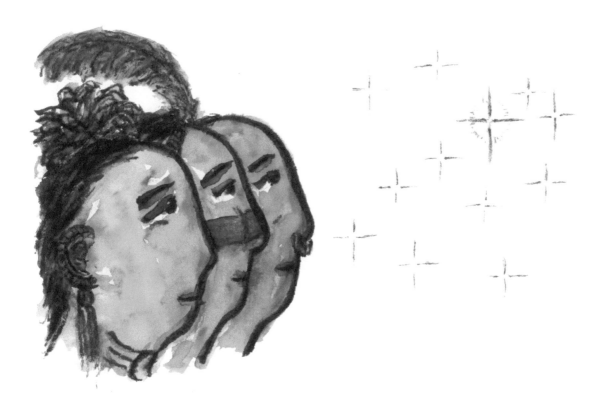

They began to ask, "Where is the one who has been born to be Grand Chief of the tribes of Wrestles With Creator? We saw his star where the sun rises and have come to bow down low before him and honor him."

When the bad hearted Chief Looks Brave, who ruled the Promised Land, heard of this he was troubled, along with all who lived in Jerusalem.

He called a council of all the chief holy men and law teachers. He asked them where the Chosen One was to be born.

"In Bethlehem, the village of Chief Much Loved One," they replied. "This is what the ancient prophecies say, 'But you Bethlehem, O House of Bread, in the land of the tribes of Wrestles With Creator, you have a good reputation, from you shall come a great chief who will guide my holy people.'"

Then Chief Looks Brave called a secret meeting with the Wisdomkeepers to find out when the star first appeared. He then sent them to the village of Chief Much Loved One and told them, "Look everywhere for the child, find him and tell me where he is, so that I may also come and bow down low before him."

Honoring
The Chosen One

When the Wisdomkeepers went their way, they saw the star rising in the East. With glad hearts they followed, until the star stopped and rested over the place where the child was.

They were welcomed into the house where they saw the child with his mother, Bitter Tears.

They bowed down low to the ground to honor the child. Then they opened their bundles and gifted him with precious gold, sweet smelling incense, and bitter ointment of Myrrh.

The Wisdomkeepers were warned in a dream not to go back to Chief Looks Brave, so they returned to their homeland by a different road.

After the Wisdomkeepers had gone a spirit messenger warned He Gives Sons in a dream.

"Rise up!" he said urgently, "take the child and his mother and go quickly to the land of Egypt and remain there until I tell you to leave. Chief Looks Brave is searching for the child to kill him!"

That night He Gives Sons took the child and his mother and fled for their lives to the land of Egypt.

They remained there until the death of Chief Looks Brave. This fulfilled the ancient prophecy, "I will bring my son from the land of Egypt."

When Chief Looks Brave realized he had been outsmarted by the Wisdomkeepers, he was full of rage and gave orders for all male children under two years of age to be put to death.

This fulfilled another age old prophecy. "A sound of weeping and wailing is heard in the high country. A woman is shedding tears for her children. No one can quiet her down, because they are no more."

The Journey Home

After Chief Looks Brave died, a spirit messenger appeared again to He Gives Sons in a dream.

He said, "Get up and take the child and his mother and go back to the land of the tribes of Wrestles With Creator. The ones who were trying to take the child's life are dead."

He Gives Sons got up, took the child and his mother and began to go where he was told. On the way, when he heard that the son of Chief Looks Brave had become the new chief, he became afraid.

After being warned in another dream, he took a different path to their home in the North hills, to an out-of-the-way village that most people looked down on, called Nazareth.

This fulfilled many ancient prophecies *such as, "He will be a small plant out of dry ground"* and *"One looked down upon,"* a Nazarene.

In this village the Holy Child grew strong in wisdom and strength, the people respected him, for the Great Spirit's power and blessing ways were resting on him.

This has been the story of the Birth of the Chosen One, retold from the Sacred Book, but this is only a small part of the story.

There is much more to be told!

Glossary of Names

Bitter Tears . . . . Mary

Chief Looks Brave . . . . King Herod

Chosen One . . . . Christ, Messiah

Creator Hears . . . . Simeon

Creator is My Promise . . . . Elizabeth

Creator is With Us . . . . Emmanuel

Creator's Mighty One . . . . Gabriel

Creator Sets Free . . . . Jesus

Creator Shows Goodwill . . . . John

Creator Will Remember . . . . Zechariah

Drawn From the Water . . . . Moses

Father of Many Nations . . . . Abraham

Great Spirit is Creator . . . . Elijah

He Gives Sons . . . . Joseph

Holy man/woman . . . . Prophet or Priest

Much Loved One . . . . David

Sacred Lodge . . . . Holy Temple

Shows Good Will . . . . Anna

Spirit Messenger . . . . Angel

Wisdomkeepers . . . . Wise Men, Magi

Wrestles With Creator . . . . Israel

First Nations Version

I hope you have enjoyed the Birth of the Chosen One.

This book is only a portion of the *First Nations Version Project* by this author. A new translation and paraphrase of the Sacred Book called the Bible.

For over twelve years my wife and I have traveled sharing our music and storytelling across North America and beyond to other nations; presenting the message of Jesus to First Nations people.

The Great Story from the Sacred Book, CD and Booklet, was our first attempt to share the story of the Bible in a culturally relevent way. In the process I began to paraphrase some of my favorite passages of Scripture to use in our live events.

The response has been favorable. Native American elders have told me, "You say it in English the way we think in our Native languages." One Elder said, "If the missionaries had told it to us like this, we would have listened long ago!"

Often, I have been asked if I was planning a paraphrase of the entire Bible. The task is, quite honestly, overwhelming but I can't deny my belief that such a translation, designed to serve Native Americans and other First Nations English speaking people is needed. With this in mind, I began this sacred journey in January of 2013.

You can find more information about this project and its status on our website, www.firstnationsversion.com.

About the Author

Terry Wildman was born and raised in lower Michigan. He is of Ojibwe (Chippewa) and Yaqui ancestry. Terry is a recording artist, songwriter, storyteller, speaker and published writer.

Terry is the "Chief" of Rain Ministries, a nonprofit organization based in Arizona. Since the year 2000 as "RainSong" he and his wife Darlene have invested their lives in sharing the message of Jesus with Native Americans.

As of this book, they have produced four music CD's, Sacred Warrior, Rising Sun, Rise Up and Dance and Hoop of Life. Their music style is a folk rock blend with Native American instruments and melodies.

In 2004 RainSong was nominated for a Grammy award and two Nammy awards. In 2005 they won the "American Christian Music Award" for the category of "Favorite Band/Duo–Breakout." In 2008 they were nominated for two Nammy Awards, one for "Best Song of the Year," All Colors Together, and for "Best Gospel Recording" for their CD Rise Up and Dance. Terry and Darlene were presenters that year at the awards ceremony held in Niagara Falls, New York.

They have also produced a storytelling CD with a musical background called *The Great Story from the Sacred Book*. This CD won the Nammy (Native American Music Award) for "Best Spoken Word" in 2009. Soon after they released a booklet to compliment the CD through Indian Life Ministries based in Manitoba, Canada, (indianlife.org).

About The Illustrator

Ramone Romero lives in Osaka, Japan, with his wife and two children.

In his own words...

I love the art that children make! Like an arrow to my heart it touches me, not because of its skill but because of their great heart.

I began painting with Jesus in 2005, and though my art wasn't very skillful, I hoped that it would have the heart and purity of children's art.

My heart is overwhelmed by the peoples, cultures, and spirituality of North American First Nations. My heart overflows, and I paint.

I am a child in understanding Native American people and culture, but I pray that my simple paintings would be a blessing of love.

With the imperfection of a child, and with all the respect and honor that I know how to give, I offer these paintings.

Ramone Romero, Cherokee and Aztec Heritage
Website: http://ramone-romero.blogspot.com

CPSIA information can be obtained
at www.ICGtesting.com
Printed in the USA
BVHW022159050821
613636BV00002B/22